A DK Publishing Book

Text Christopher Maynard
Project Editor Jane Donnelly
Art Editor Melanie Whittington
Deputy Managing Art Editor Jane Horne
Deputy Managing Editor Mary Ling
Production Ruth Cobb
Consultant Theresa Greenaway
Picture Researcher Tom Worsley

Additional photography by David Murray, Stephen Shott, David Johnson, Peter Chadwick, Dave King, Stephen Oliver, Ian O'Leary, Tim Ridley, Geoff Dann, Andy Crawford, Philip Dowell, Peter Anderson, Jane Burton, Mike Dunning

First American Edition, 1997
2 4 6 8 10 9 7 5 3
Published in the United States by
DK Publishing, Inc., 95 Madison Avenue, New York, New York 10016
Visit us on the World Wide Web at http://www.dk.com

Copyright © 1997 Dorling Kindersley Limited, London

Color reproduction by Chromagraphics, Singapore.
Printed and bound in Italy by L.E.G.O.

The publisher would like to thank the following for their kind permission to reproduce their photographs:
t top, b bottom, l left, r right, c center, BC back cover, FC front cover
The Anthony Blake Photo Library: (Why does gelatin wobble?)cr, crb, title page cb, (Why does gelatin wobble?)tl; **Cephas Picture Library:** (Why does gelatin wobble?)cl; **Tony Stone Images:** Paul Chesley BC c, (Why does rice ...?)c, Peter Correz (Why do some people eat ...?)c, Nick Gunderson (Why don't the eggs ...?)br, David Olsen (Why are pineapples prickly?)c, FC, Joel Papavoine endpapers, Christel Rosenfeld (Why do some things taste sweet?)c, Andy Sacks (Why do apples have cores?)c, (Why is fruit good for me?)br, Don Smetzer (Why is fruit good for me?)c, Joe Solem FC c, Denis Waugh (Why does rice ...?)br, Zane Williams (Why are pineapples prickly?)bl; **Zefa Pictures:** (Why does gelatin wobble?)bl

Questions

Why does gelatin wobble?

Why do some things taste sweet?

Why does rice grow underwater?

Why do apples have cores?

Why is fruit good for me?

Why are pineapples prickly?

Why do some people eat more than others?

Why don't the eggs we eat have chicks inside?

WHY

are pineapples prickly?

Questions children ask about food

A gelatin dessert combines proteins and hot water. They bond together and form a solid as the water cools. But the bonds are weak, so the gelatin wobbles.

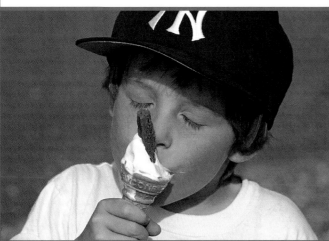

Why does ice cream melt?
Ice cream is a mixture of eggs, sugar, cream, and flavorings

wobble?

Why are there bubbles in some drinks? Bubbles of carbon dioxide can be forced into a drink at the factory to make it fizzy. When you open the drink, the bubbles start to escape.

that is frozen into its solid state. Just like snow, if it is exposed to heat, it will turn back to liquid.

Sweet food contains lots of sugar. When it touches taste buds on your tongue, messages are sent to your brain, which tells you of the flavor.

Why are chilies hot?
They're not hot to touch, but if you bite one, the chemicals inside irritate and burn your mouth.

taste sweet?

**Why are
lemons sour?**
Citrus fruits, such as lemons,
limes, grapefruit, and oranges,
all contain a small amount
of citric acid in their juices.
Citric acid
tastes sour.

Why do chips make me thirsty?
Salt absorbs water. If you eat salty chips, your
mouth tells your brain that you need a drink.

Why does rice grow

Rice is a type of grass that needs warm weather and lots of water to grow. Rice is planted in flooded fields to give the plants all the moisture they need to produce rice grains. The fields are drained before the rice is harvested.

Why do some peas hide in pods?
Peas are pea plant seeds, and grow in pods like beans. We eat most seeds and

Why do apples

Cores contain pips, apple tree seeds. The juicy apples are eaten by animals and birds, who then scatter the pips in their droppings.

Why are potatoes dirty?
Potatoes are swollen parts of a potato plant's stems

underwater?

Why is tea brown?
Tea is made by soaking tea leaves in hot water. The leaves contain chemical substances called tannins, which dissolve in the water. Tannins are used to make dyes – in this case, they dye the water brown.

pods together, but pea pods can be too thick and tough, so we take the peas out.

have cores?

Why do peaches have pits inside?
A pit is the tough case that protects a peach seed from greedy insects. If a pit is planted, the seed inside may sprout and start to grow.

that form underground to store nutrients for the plant. These swellings are called tubers. We dig them up, wash, then cook them.

Why is fruit good

Fruit is rich in the vitamins and minerals we need to keep us healthy.

Why does fruit change color?
As the seeds inside a fruit mature, chemicals in the fruit change its color. The color signals to animals when the fruit is ready to eat, and they then scatter the ripe seeds.

for me?

Fruit also contains plenty of fiber, which helps our digestion.

Why do we wash fruit and vegetables?
Fruit and vegetables are sprayed with chemicals to keep away insects. We wash off these chemicals, and peel skin that is too tough to eat.

Why are pineapples

Pineapple
leaves have
spiny edges
to stop animals
from eating them.
But birds cling to and
eat the spiky fruit, then
carry away the seeds.

**Why do farmers flood
cranberry fields?**
The fields are flooded in order

prickly?

Why are raisins wrinkly?
Raisins are actually dried grapes. As they lose water, they shrivel up and shrink and their skin turns wrinkly and brown.

to harvest the berries. They are shaken loose, then float to the surface to be gathered.

Why are coconuts so rough?
The hard shell and rough, hairy layer of a coconut help keep the milk and flesh inside from drying out.

Why do some people

Grown-ups eat more than children because their bigger bodies need more energy. Some people, like athletes, need to eat lots of food since they use up a huge amount of energy when they exercise.

Why do onions make me cry?
When we slice an onion it gives off strong chemicals that sting

eat more than others?

Why are carrots good for our eyes?
The vitamin A in carrots helps make sure our vision stays good. Bet you've never seen a rabbit wearing glasses!

our eyes. Our eyes fill with tears to wash out the chemicals.

Why don't the eggs

Eggs from stores never have chicks inside them because they have not been fertilized by

Why do we call them hamburgers?
This popular food came to the US from Hamburg, a city in Germany. In the US, it was put inside a bun and covered with ketchup.

ve eat have chicks inside?

a rooster. A fertilized egg would be kept warm so that the chick inside could grow and hatch.

Why don't fruit trees grow inside me?
You might accidentally swallow a fruit seed, but it will pass straight through your body, or your digestive juices will break it down.